FERTIG TO FERTICK

Following the Family Name from
Germany to Jerecho

SCOTT FERTICK

Fertig to Fertick:
Following the Family Name from Germany to Jerecho
by Scott Fertick

Copyright © 2025
All rights reserved.
Published by the Author

All rights reserved. Reproduction or utilization of this work in any form, by any means now known or herein after invented, including but not limited to xerography, photocopying and recording, and in any storage and retrieval system, is forbidden without permission from the copyrighted holder.

International Standard Book Number: 978-1-60126-997-3

Masthof Press
219 Mill Road | Morgantown, PA 19543-9516
www.Masthof.com

TABLE OF CONTENTS

Introduction v

1. Challenges 1
2. Origins of the Name 5
3. Germany 9
4. Four Generations in Germany 15
5. John Sr. 21
6. John Jr. 31
7. Jacob Sr. 37
8. Jacob Jr. 43
9. Albert 49
10. Roscoe Sr. 53
11. Roscoe Jr. 59
12. Scott 65
13. Jacob 71
14. Jerecho & the Future 77

Appendix 79

Introduction

The purpose of this book is to provide a simple but accurate path that follows a specific branch of the Fertick, formerly Fertig, family tree. Family trees have many branches, and the further you go back, the more those branches expand and often become difficult to follow. This knowledge of the past can be rewarding and exciting as more and more history is uncovered. It can also be overwhelming trying to fit all that knowledge into one small collection. For that reason, the intent here is to follow the Fertig/Fertick name lineally, as it has passed down over the generations from the earliest known family members in Germany, to the original American immigrants, to the newest member of the family line, Jerecho Fertick Schumacher.

The family has long been aware of the name of the original immigrant to America, John (Johannes) Fertig, who emigrated from Germany in 1754. Knowledge of the family prior to that time proved to be more elusive. This book will explore that missing information, going back to the family in Germany as accurately and as far as possible, all the while hoping to avoid too much speculation. As the lines progress into America, other branches and family members will be mentioned, of course, but ultimately it will continue to follow the name lineally from Johannes (one of many by that name) to Jerecho.

Much of the information included here has been drawn from documents and records already in the possession of the Fertick family, followed by an attempt to navigate the world of online genealogy to fill in gaps and find new records, to the extent that those records can be trusted. There is no pretense here to being an in-depth, academic study, with the author delving through mountains of church records in dusty archive rooms in Germany. Those records do exist, however, and some of the information discovered there by other researchers has been recorded online and added here to the family story with much appreciation. The goal is to take this known and newly found information and transcribe it into an easily read narrative that makes future contemplation of the family history considerably less tedious.

As anyone who has researched genealogy can attest, there are many challenges to tracing a family's roots. In the case of the Fertick family, it appears that one unfortunate member was swindled by a well-known genealogical fraud who created an amazing and realistic history of the family. This fraudulent history has taken root due to the apparent quality of the research and fascinating collection of soldiers and nobility. As a result, it is not hard to find genealogical sites with private family trees that enthusiastically follow this idealistic family line, causing confusion for future generations.

These variations will be discussed, with the goal of compiling the most accurate genealogy possible with the information at hand. There has never been any doubt regarding the family line from the immigrant, John Fertig, until the present time. The trick is to find where the true family history and the falsified version converge prior to his emigration. It appears that this divergence originates with his parents, so one does not have to go far to find it.

A note on names. This family tree, like many others, has several names that are passed down over generations to honor aunts, uncles and grandparents, and quite a few instances where names are carried down directly from father to son. The immigrant John had a son named John. It was a common name throughout all the branches of the family, and it turns out that the four generations prior to John in Germany were also all named John (Johannes). The next two generations after John's son were both named Jacob, and there is also a pair named Roscoe. In those instances, the names will be simplified to John Sr. and John Jr., Jacob Sr. and Jacob Jr., and Roscoe Sr. and Roscoe Jr. to provide clarity when names occasionally blend together in the narrative.

The hope is that this book will be passed down through the years so that current and future generations of the Fertick family, including Jerecho and his future cousins and relatives, will know the generations that came before and remember them fondly.

Challenges

A study of the genealogy of this branch of the Fertick family starts, ironically, with an individual who is in no way related to the family. That individual is one Gustave Anjou, who lived from 1863 to 1942. Why would a Swedish man with a French-sounding name be so important to the genealogy of a family from Germany that migrated to America? The unfortunate answer is that Mr. Anjou appears to be the main source of an abundance of misinformation that continues to haunt the family line, and likely a source of financial pain to whichever member of the Fertick family commissioned him to research the family history. His part in the story originates with the discovery of two genealogical works found in obscure parts of the country, which have lured many an amateur genealogist down a misleading path.

The first of these works was discovered in the San Diego Regional Genealogical Library and titled *History of the Fertig (De La Ferte, Fertich) Family.* There was no author or date listed. The Fertick name is not common and even less so west of the Mississippi River, however, a small contingent of Ferticks can be found in California. The Fertig surname is more common, so the location is not as unusual as it may initially seem. The information in this work closely matches information found in a second work discovered in the Fort Wayne Library in Indiana. Again, there is evidence of Fertigs who relocated to Indiana from Pennsylvania. In fact, one grandson of the immigrant, John Fertig, is believed to have passed away in Wayne County, Indiana.

The book found in the Fort Wayne Library can be found online. It was transcribed by Pat Frappier from Kettering, Ohio, in 1986. In her transcription, Ms. Frappier states that she found a note indicating that the pages she discovered appeared to be photocopied in 1973 from documents found in the Goodspeed Book Shop in Boston, Massachusetts. Another researcher, John C. Fertick, wrote a letter to the bookshop in 1986 asking about the book. In their response, they said they did not have the book, but did have a citation. The book was listed as *Fertig Family of Germany and France, From Antoine De La Ferte, 1487 to Christopher Fertig of Pennsylvania 1774*, by G. Anjou. So here enters our mysterious Gustave Anjou.

Gustave Anjou's manuscript has been printed as anonymous by several publishers who were unaware of the fraudulent nature of the work.

From the reference to the De La Ferte family in both books, and from the similarities throughout, it became clear that both these documents came from the same source. The fact that the bookstore had the citation is helpful. The information provided traces the family from the immigrant, John, back to the De La Ferte family in France, as far as the wedding of Antoine De La Ferte in 1487 as the title indicates. The history of the family shows a connection to French nobility, marriages in the grandest of churches, war heroes and eventual religious persecution that led the family to migrate to Germany. The name changes as they relocate from De La Ferte to Ferte to Fertich and finally to Fertig. The book is full of impressive references and documentation almost too good to be true and therefore extremely believable to those who want to believe. Therein lies the problem. The nobility, the list of distinguished ancestors, and the impressive documentation are the trademarks of Gustave Anjou.

Anjou was born in Sweden. His birthname was Gustaf Ludvig Jungberg. Not surprisingly, he spent time in prison for forgery in his twenties. After his release, he had various aliases, eventually taking his fiancé's maiden name as his own, becoming Gustave Anjou. He and his wife immigrated to the United States where he continued his career in forgery, taking on the persona of a professional genealogist. He might have made good as a professional actor because he played the part to perfection and earned the trust of many wealthy clients. He lived in New York City where there was money to spare and many families who were receptive to the pedigrees he discovered for them.

He was successful for several reasons. His research was extensive and backed up by impressive documentation. The citations were a common feature of his works, along with connections to events and people that would appeal to those who sought out his services. Back in those days, trying to fact check his work would be virtually impossible and because he produced exactly what his clients

A portrait of Gustave Anjou.

desired, why would they want to fact check? The asking price for his services was exorbitant for the time, and he became very well off as a result. It was not until the 1990s and the rise of internet genealogy that his works started to come into question, and it was not long before he was proven to be a very talented fraud.

Which Fertick or Fertig requested his services and when is unknown, but it would make sense that it was during the early 1900s when Anjou was at the peak of his career and charging his highest prices. His work on the Fertig family history was clearly designed to trace the European background of the immigrant, John, as the work ends with him and his immediate family and tells of an impressive heritage going back to France. There is no reason to discuss that history here in detail as it is not relevant to the actual history of the Fertig family, which is decidedly more stationary. The Fertig family in Germany did not move around much until John immigrated to America with his mother and stepfather. For the sake of curiosity, the De La Ferte family tree as presented by Gustave Anjou is included in the Appendix at the end of this book.

With the reasons for the contradictory accounts of the family tree now understood, it is possible to move on to the true history of the Fertig/Fertick family line. Before getting to the individuals, however, a little time should be taken to look at the origins of the Fertig surname as they can best be determined.

2

Origins of the Name

The literal origin of the name Fertig is not difficult to determine. It is a German word that came to be used as a surname. When and how it came to be used for that purpose is open to speculation. Looking at the German definition of *fertig*, there is no specific trait or occupation that is a sure origin since there are quite a few meanings and variations. There are some amusing and lesser used definitions. For the sake of family history, hopefully the use of the word to describe a deadbeat is not the original trait applied to an ancestor. Another amusing phrase is "*Und fertig*," which is a variation of "Bob's your uncle!" This is a British term, and after some research, it turns out that it can be translated as "and there you have it" or "it's done."

Translating the phrase as "it's done" comes closest to the most common definition. The multiple definitions listed for *fertig* in a German dictionary are due to several phrases that include the word, so it is best to look for a short and precise definition as it stands alone. The word *fertig* means ready, finished, complete, or through. Another good definition is ready-to-use, which is often combined with other words to describe finished goods and products. This could be a clue to the oft used method of a surname being determined by a person's profession.

In 1983, a gentleman named Josef Fertig wrote an article for the local newspaper in Bensheim, Germany, the *Bergstrasser Hematblatter*, which he entitled "Der Familiename Fertig." In English, "The

The Main River near Miltenberg in Lower Franconia, Germany. Dock workers may have yelled "fertig," or ready, when ferries would prepare to depart and cross the river. (photo: Scirocco340/Shutterstock)

Family Name Fertig." He speculates that one possible origin for the last name could be from dock workers who would yell, *"Fertig!"* when ferries were getting ready to depart and cross the Main River. This is just one example as it would seem reasonable to assume that there were many occupations where a worker may want to warn bystanders or co-workers to be ready or keep an eye out for a potentially dangerous situation. And then there is the aforementioned possibility that because the word can also be used to describe finished goods, a manufacturer of such goods could also have taken on that surname.

In his article, Mr. Fertig states that while the name Fertig can still be found in the area around Bensheim, it is not common as most people with that name emigrated to the United States over the previous 150 years. According to the website Forebears.io, data from 2014 shows the surname Fertig was found in 2,572 incidences in the United States and only 2,171 in Germany, so despite the German origins the name is now more common in America. The surname Fertick is even less common. There were only 53 instances of this specific spelling of the name in 2014, all in the United States.

There are many variations of both Fertig and Fertick. Often this is the result of handwritten church and census records that the original clerk either misunderstood or misprinted, or incorrect reading of the names by later genealogists. Sometimes the variations are simply the result of linguistic and geographic interpretation as families migrated from one area to another. Mr. Fertig touches on several of these variations. From the area of Tyrol, in modern-day Austria, there were the Ferdik and Ferdigg families. There is the Russian name Fertschnigg that he feels is not relevant in this case. There were also Fertiggs who came to Germany from Pomerania, in modern-day Germany and Poland, to escape from Frederick the Great in the 1750s. The name Fortig was found in 1772 to be used occasionally by Fertigs around Benzheimer and a Joseph Fertich was mentioned in 1764 in that same vicinity.

The variations of the name and possible places of origin are many, but most examples above date after or coincide with the immigration of John Fertig, so while interesting, they are not relevant to the family tree. John migrated to America in 1754, and his branch of the family can be traced back to the same area in Germany going back to 1594. They did not move around and if they did immigrate to Germany at some point in the past, that information is lost. Josef Fertig does touch on an interesting character, however, who may be relevant to John's lineage.

In a book entitled *The History of the Cloisters of Amorbach in the 14th and 15th Centuries* by Richard Koreas, he found reference to Beringer Fertig who was the schoolmaster of Cloister Amorbach in the early 1400s. The first reference to Beringer Fertig was from the University of Heidleberg in 1390 where he used the Latinized name Berngerus Vertig. The records do not indicate that he was a student, so it appears that he worked there and had received his baccalaureate degree from another university, since the University of Heidelberg did not open until 1386. He was educated early in life at the Cloister Amorbach and returned there as schoolmaster following his time at the university. He was also a lawyer, having signed off on a legal document between the cloister and local farmers regarding the tithing of crops.

Cloister Amorbach where Beringer Fertig was educated and later returned as schoolmaster.

Joseph Fertig believes Beringer Fertig was the first person to legally document the name Fertig. It seems safer to say that his was the first known legally documented use of the name as there may be others where we simply do not have records. There is a reference at the time to a Count Fertig. Whether he was related to Beringer or in any way connected is unknown. What is relevant to the immigrant, John Fertig, who was born three hundred years later, is location.

Germany

In the account written by Gustave Anjou, John Fertig's genealogy can be traced back seven generations to a wedding in Pas de Calais, France, in 1487. Antoine De Le Ferte married a noble lady in a beautiful monastery and what follows is a winding path eventually leading to Germany. The actual family history is considerably more settled. Beringer Fertig lived in Amorbach, which is in the Lower Franconia region of Bavaria. To the northeast of Amorbach, across the Main River and roughly twenty miles as the crow flies, lies the village of Altfeld, the birthplace of not only the immigrant, John, but also of all his known predecessors.

Bavaria is one of sixteen modern German states. It covers the entire southeast corner of the country and borders Baden-Wurttemberg to the west. The extreme northwest corner of Bavaria sticks out to the west, nestled in between Baden to the south and the state of Hesse to the north. This corner is a

Map of Germany. The area where Altfeld is located is circled.

part of Lower Franconia, and where the early Fertig family is found. A large portion of this corner sits in a U-shaped section of land, the sides of the U being formed by the Main River. On the right side of that U, near the western shore is Altfeld. The location of Altfeld, so close to Amorbach, certainly hints at a possible connection to Beringer Fertig. Despite sharing the surname, however, there is no way to reliably confirm any such lineage, so it is speculation at best.

Present-day Altfeld is a small village surrounded by patchwork farmland that occasionally makes space for other equally small villages. A short walk west from Altfeld leads to the Village of Michelrieth, where the family likely attended the local Lutheran church. Several relevant family records have been found in that church. A further short walk west will lead to the Village of Schollbrunn, where John Fertig's wife Elizabeth was born and raised. It is a relatively small area, but all the known references to this branch of the Fertig family are contained in this scenic area. To the west and across the Main River to the south around Amorbach is the low, forested mountain region called the Odenwald.

Trying to find information online about Altfeld can be a challenge because being so small, most references tend to point out places "near" Altfeld rather than the village itself. The west side of town is dominated by a Proctor and Gamble manufacturing plant, which is obviously a recent addition. Even now, looking at a map gives the impression of a quiet village life. The Odenwald, however, is a popular tourist area so it is likely that a portion of that tourism finds its way to the villages in and around Altfeld. All in all, it appears to be a beautiful area, so despite Gustave Anjou's tales of a grand odyssey from France, it is easy to see the appeal to several generations of a family in simply staying put. The Fertig family prior to John's immigration certainly did just that.

A misty scene in the Odenwald Forest. (photo: Steven Heb)

Despite that beauty, in the 1700s emigration from the area became more common and preferred by many villagers. To understand why, it is necessary to examine the political situation more than the geography. Altfeld was in the Circle of Franconia, which was created in 1500. Imperial circles were the equivalent of states in the Holy Roman Empire. Within this Circle, Altfeld was part of the County of Wertheim, which was governed by the Counts of Wertheim. When that line died off, the area was reassigned to the Counts of Lowenstein. In 1754, the certificates of manumission, which freed peasants from vassalage to their local lords and were required prior to emigrating, were dictated by "His Highness Prince and Lord, Sir Carl, Reigning Prince of Lowenstein-Wertheim in the Holy Roman Empire."

There were many reasons why life could be hard on villagers in Wertheim. Wertheim was a small Protestant state situated between two Catholic states at a time when religious tensions were high. War was constant. The locals had already suffered from a twenty-year feud with Catholic rival, Wurzburg, and that was followed by the Thirty

Years' War, an essentially religious war between Catholic and Protestant rivals throughout Europe and one of the most brutal wars in history. The war ran from 1618 to 1648. Afterwards, locals still had to deal with incursions from French kings, so there was a constant movement of troops in the area over the years. Both foreign and local troops required money and provisions, and typically abused locals who had the misfortune of being stuck between them.

Vassalage and living in a feudal land also took its toll. Vassals were given land to work by local lords who required a vow of homage and loyalty. The lords could dictate long work hours and taxes on their vassals' property and crops. A list of taxes provided in Volume 12 of The Pennsylvania German Folklore Society, even without much explanation of what they entailed, gives an idea of the conditions and subsequent poverty suffered by many vassals. In addition to the required labor, there were grazing fees, hunting fees, watch fees, pannage, plowing fees, dyeing fees, food tax, personal tax for the prince, chimney tax, water tax, tithes, ground rents and more. This is not the full list but a sample. The lords could provide leniency in some cases if they chose, but the demands were still greater than most vassals could afford.

Even when a person wished to emigrate, it was not an easy matter. To get a request for manumission one would need to pay a clerk to write the petition. The fees required by the lords to grant manumission could vary but were occasionally waived, either from generosity or simply to rid the villages of less than desirable residents. Some people attempted to escape from the area without paying any fees. The fees typically had more to do with the amount of property owned than with any value assigned to the individual. In the 1700s, when emigration started to become a problem for the lords due to loss of labor, restrictions and deterrents were created. An individual who emigrated was expected to stay away and would not be granted citizenship if they returned, and taxes on movable property began to increase for those wishing to leave.

    Measures like these did eventually slow the tide of emigration, especially after 1755, but John Fertig and his family emigrated in 1754 in the last large surge. Before we focus on him, however, it is time to look at the four generations prior to his departure who lived and stayed in the area under these conditions.

4

Four Generations in Germany

Tracking the family history to just one location and finding a traditional family that shared names from generation to generation is not going to produce a Gustave Anjou level of excitement, but the truth is always better than fiction. That is exactly what a search of the German Fertig family finds. The names Johannes, John and Hans are one and the same. Johannes is common, Hans can refer to a younger member of the family sharing the name with the father, and John is the anglicized version. The immigrant, John, went by Johannes in Germany. So did all his direct ascendants from the four generations before him. Every one of them was born, lived, and died in Altfeld.

In Chapter 1, it was a John C. Fertig who was able to procure the citation for Gustave Anjou's work from a bookstore in Boston. This may be the same John Christian Fertig who hired a professional genealogist from Munich to look at the registers at Michelrieth Lutheran Church, where several family records were found. As mentioned earlier, Michelrieth is just a short walk from Altfeld. The records go back to the birth of Johannes Fertig in Altfeld around 1594. This is the first known Fertig ancestor in the line and there is not much information beyond that. He married Anna and died in Altfeld in either 1671 or 1672. The years of the wedding, Anna's birth, and her death are approximated over decades, so it is safe to say those dates have been lost to time. What is known, and already hinted at, is that they had a son named Johannes.

The Lutheren church in Michelrieth where several family records were located. (photo: Flodur63)

Johannes Fertig was born in Altfeld around 1624. He married Catharina Friudenberger on June 14, 1663, in Altfeld. Like the rest of the family, they seemingly spent their entire lives in Altfeld where Johannes passed away around 1700. Like his mother, the dates of his wife's birth and death are unknown, so it is somewhat surprising to have such an exact date for the wedding. It would be convenient for the dates to start coming into more clarity, but as seen with their son, yet another Johannes Fertig, that is not the case.

The third Johannes was born on March 9 in either 1667 or 1668 in Altfeld. There is once again a specific date for a wedding. Johannes married Christina Albert on April 23, 1689, in Altfeld. For whatever reason, the church records were specific for marriages, but birth dates and deaths were harder to come by. In this case, Johannes' death is estimated to have occurred between 1703 and 1759, so the actual date is unknown, as are the dates of birth and death for his wife, Christina. There are more specific dates for their son and finally a slight variation in the name. He was born Hans Peter Fertig, although

Aerial view of Altfeld, Germany. (photo: Axel Hasler)

Hans is just another version of Johannes. In this case, however, the addition of the middle name, Peter, is telling in determining the true family origin of John the immigrant.

Hans Peter Fertig was born on March 13, 1699, or 1700, in Altfeld. The records, as can be seen, regularly show two years, so it is one or the other and unclear why they are listed that way. Hans married Anna Gerberich on June 22, 1728, in Altfeld. Anna was born on January 30 or 31, 1708 or 1709 in Altfeld. In the church records from their wedding, Hans was listed as a master tailor. They had four children, all born in Altfeld. Apollonia Fertig was born on August 17, 1729, Peter Fertig on February 22, 1730 or 1731, and Michael Fertig on October 3, 1732. Their youngest child, Hans Mathias Fertig, the immigrant, was born on February 24, 1736. It is here, with Hans Peter and his wife, Anna, that a great deal of confusion comes in regarding this family line. A big part of this is that Gustave Anjou selected a different set of parents for the immigrant. Another is the unfortunate fact that on

November 20, 1737, Hans Peter Fertig passed away in Altfeld when his youngest son was not even two years old.

There are three reasons for the confusion. Gustave Anjou is the first and most obvious. He lists the parents of John Fertig, the immigrant, as Adam Fertig and Johanna Haupt from Diedesheim, Germany. Even if the known fraudulent nature of Anjou's work was not enough, the names of the actual parents give a clue to the true genealogy. As mentioned, the name Hans Peter Fertig is important. When John immigrated to America and eventually married, he named one of his sons John Peter, a nod to his biological father. The second reason for the confusion is that his mother remarried. On April 19, 1738, not long after Hans Peter passed away, Anna married Johann Adam Sauer, which brings up another interesting sidenote regarding names. John was born Hans Mathias Fertig, but after settling in America he went by Hans Adam Fertig. His son was named after his biological father. It is possible the change from Mathias to Adam was a nod to his stepfather, Johann Adam, but that is just speculation.

The third source of confusion comes from the name of the ship John and his family traveled on to immigrate to America. There is no debate that John Fertig immigrated to America on the ship *Phoenix* out of Rotterdam, commanded by John Spurrier. The question is when. The same ship arrived in America on November 2, 1752, and on October 1, 1754. It can be safely assumed this ship made the trip on multiple occasions, but these two dates are significant. The passenger list from 1752 includes a Hans Fertig and this is often assumed to be the immigrant, John. To add some confusion, records from the Pennsylvania German Folklore Society show that this Hans was a tailor's son. John's biological father was a tailor. But looking further into the records, this Hans was in debt and wished to immigrate to New England with his wife. John was only sixteen at that time and was not married, so he was not the Hans from 1752.

When the *Phoenix* sailed in 1754, the passenger list included the Sauer family. John's mother, Anna, is not listed but women were not usually listed on the passenger lists at that time. From the Sauer family, the list includes Johannes Sauer, Hans Adam Sauer, Hans Michael Sauer, and Johann Michael Sauer. The names can be confusing because they all include a form of John, but it appears these four are the stepfather, Johann Adam Sauer, his son Adam Sauer, and the two stepsons, John and Michael who were listed under their stepfather's last name. The list also includes Andreas Fertig and Lorenz Albert, who were known cousins of John.

The record of the Pennsylvania German Folklore Society includes a letter from Michael Fertig to Lorenz Albert from June 30, 1782, that backs up this information. It reads, "Beloved Friend and Esteemed Cousin Lorentz Albert…My stepbrother Adam Sauer lives nearby here, and his father with him. Mother has been dead two years…My brother, Johannas Fertig, lives in Chester County about 18 miles from me in Est Nentmel (East Nantmeal) Township, has a wife and six children, 100 or more acres of land, but is not getting on….Besides, I wanted to inquire of you, if I may, whether you could not give me some news of our cousin Andreas Fertig."

This letter, along with the list of passengers from 1754, seems to verify the 1754 immigration timeline. It also confirms that Anna Sauer passed away in 1780 in Pennsylvania. The most obvious clue to the immigration date comes from John Fertig himself. His tombstone in Brownback Cemetery in Pennsylvania says that he immigrated in 1754. There are genealogies that try to pass this off as an error in efforts to confirm the 1752 timeline but in this case benefit of the doubt seems not only reasonable, but also appropriate. So, it is in 1754 that we can begin the American history of the Fertig family.

John Sr.

The life of the immigrant, Johannes Fertig, has been touched on already and often. In America, he went by John and moving forward he will occasionally be referred to as John Sr. to avoid confusion with his son, John Jr., who is next in the direct line following the Fertig name. John Sr. was born on February 24, 1736, in Altfeld. His father died in 1737, and his mother remarried the next year. It was with this new family that he came to America in 1754. His older biological siblings, Apollonia and Peter, do not appear to have come to America with the rest of the family. He came across the ocean with his stepfather, mother, stepbrother Adam, and his biological brother Michael. When they arrived in Philadelphia on October 1, Michael was two days shy of his twenty-second birthday, and John was seventeen.

There is no specific evidence indicating the condition of John and his family in Germany. Not everyone was under the condition of vassalage, but even those who were not were still subject to fees and taxes. The family member and fellow immigrant with the best surviving documentation is his cousin Lorenz Albert, who was a passenger on the *Phoenix* with John. Lorenz Albert was a cartwright and was under vassalage prior to emigrating from Germany. A cartwright made and repaired carts and wagons, along with various carpentry jobs. He appeared before the local government court on May 13, 1754, and declared that he could not support himself in his trade any

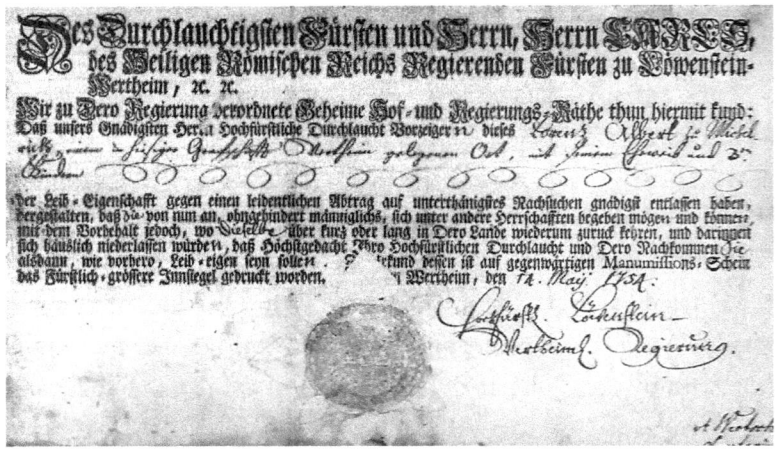

Letter of Manumission written for Lorenz Albert in 1756.

more since every farmer typically made his own plows. In his plea he states, "It is no impertinence or desire of mine, which drives me from the country, but poverty and uneasiness over wife and child."

Lorenz's petition was successful. His Letter of Manumission, granted the next day, still exists in the records of his descendants. After "a most humble petition and in return for a tolerable sum," he was released from vassalage along with his wife, Anna Barbara, and his three children. The family then made plans to join the Sauers, with John Fertig, and another cousin, Andreas Fertig to travel down the Main River to Rotterdam, and from there find a ship to take them to America. It is interesting to note that despite laws to discourage emigration by refusing to allow emigrants who return to become citizens, the Letter of Manumission specifically states that if the Alberts were to return, they would be welcomed back but be returned to vassalage. It appears that Lorenz Albert had a good reputation with the local lord.

The trip down river likely started with a wagon trip from Altfeld to Wertheim, where the families would find boats for the trip on the

Main River. The Main eventually joined the Rhine, and the boats followed the various branches of the Rhine delta to Rotterdam in the Netherlands. Albert family tradition implies this family group made their own arrangements for travel, but there were emigration agents that worked for "shipmen" and paid by the head to entice emigrants. Some shipmen were authorized by the government for this purpose, but others had questionable ethics, and those were occasionally indicted by the government for fraud. The trip down the river could take three to four weeks and passed much history along the way. A wonderful, albeit fictionalized, account of the emigration of the family can be found in the book *Little Pilgrim to Penn's Woods*, written by Edna Albert, the great, great-granddaughter of Lorenz Albert. Written from the perspective of a young girl, the book is full of family stories passed down generations about the original immigrants to America.

Due to the unpredictability of traveling across the Atlantic Ocean in a sail ship, the time required could vary considerably. Four

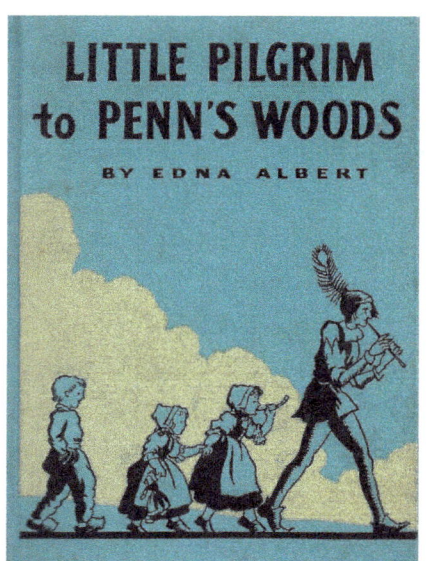

Little Pilgrim to Penn's Woods *was written by Edna Albert and is a fictionalized account of the move to America by the Fertig and Albert families.*

weeks would be a fortunate trip, but it could take up to seven. Any more than that and the already questionable conditions could become much worse. The immigrants had to pay their share for provisions provided by the ship and for any personal provisions they brought along. There was always a chance of losing property to theft, violence, or dishonesty. Sanitary conditions were a challenge and would likely worsen the longer the voyage took. Disease was always a fear and as one can imagine on a ship full of as many as five hundred typically land-based passengers, seasickness was prevalent. In Edna Albert's book, Lorenz Albert loses a young daughter at sea, and that may be based on actual family memories considering that not everybody survived the trip. It was especially hard on young children.

When the *Phoenix* arrived in Philadelphia, John and all the other male passengers over the age of sixteen were walked down Chestnut Street to the Pennsylvania State House where they were required to give the oath of allegiance to King George II. This is the Pennsylvania State House that eventually became Independence Hall; home of the Liberty Bell, where the Declaration of Independence and U.S. Constitution were written, and which served as the national capitol for a time. One must wonder if John ever felt a sense of irony later in life regarding taking the oath in that building. In 1781 he served in the army during the Revolutionary War against England.

Despite traveling under the name of their stepfather, Sauer, Michael and John kept the name Fertig in America. John settled in Vincent Township in Chester County and seems to have stayed in Chester County for most of his life. Michael lived in Chester County initially but eventually moved north to the area around Harrisburg. Both John and Michael were married at New Hanover Lutheran Church. The church was built from logs in 1700, and the brothers were married in that original building. A new church built of stone was raised in 1768 and the church still stands on the foundation of that stone building. Michael married Anna Marie Reis on June 10, 1764. John had married Elizabeth Deihm two years earlier on September 12, 1762.

Elizabeth Deihm was born on October 17, 1739, in Schollbrunn, Germany, to Hans Adam Deihm and Margaretha Deihm. She and her parents came over from Germany on the *Phoenix* at the same time as John's family. There are, as usual, various dates and even ships listed depending on the genealogy, but a look at the 1754 passenger list verifies that they were on the same ship. Like Fertig, there are several people with the last name Deihm who emigrated in the 1750s, which likely adds to the confusion. There is also an alternate date for John and Elizabeth's wedding, October 24, but that they got married in the fall of 1762 is not in dispute. They lived together in East Nantmeal, also in Chester County.

John and Elizabeth had seven children. The first appears to have been John Jr., the next in the direct line being followed here. He was born on September 6, 1763. There is a genealogy that shows the year of birth as 1762, but this would have been ten days before John and Elizabeth got married so appears to be an error. Another shows the year 1768, which would make him their second child, but John Jr.'s first child was born in 1786 when he would have been only seventeen years old. The confusion may simply arise because the final number of his date of birth on his otherwise well-preserved tombstone is faded and could be a 3 or 8, but 1763 is the correct date by any reasonable consideration, making him the firstborn child.

The second child was John Peter Fertig, named after John Sr.'s biological father. He was born on September 6, 1766. Mary Fertig was born on January 25, 1767. There is not a lot known about Mary and she is left off some lists of the children. Some genealogists have speculated that she may have passed away at a young age, but there is evidence that she was alive as of 1782, which will be elaborated on shortly. The fourth and fifth children are Adam Fertig and Abraham Fertig. Adam was born in 1770. Abraham may have been born on November 4, 1769, or alternately 1771. The sixth child, Jacob Fertig, was born on September 9, 1778. The seventh and last child was Elizabeth Fertig, born on July 20, 1784.

The letter from Michael Fertig to Lorenz Albert, written in 1782, stated that John Sr. had a wife and six children. Their seventh child was not born until 1784, which confirms that Mary was still alive at the time. Taking facts from various sources, it is possible to formulate a timeline for her. Harmon Aughe was born in Pennsylvania and married to a Mary Magdalene Fertig. Some genealogies show that she was born in Virginia but that is unlikely. Harmon had two wives during his lifetime, and his connection to other members of John Sr.'s family is supported by the fact that John Jr. married into a local Aughe family. Putting the information together it appears that Harmon Aughe married Mary Fertig, who died early in the marriage. Harmon's first child, born on December 4, 1788, was named John Fertig Aughe. He does not have any other children until 1803, fifteen years later by which time he would have remarried, so there is enough in these combined records to feel comfortable that this Mary was the daughter of John and Elizabeth.

John Sr. and his family arrived in America shortly before the outbreak of the French and Indian War, which pitted England against France. Both countries antagonized local Indian tribes to join their cause. Edna Albert touches briefly in her book on the fears of immigrant settlers as the various tribes went on the warpath. Following the war, the British required all male colonists from the age of 16 to 45 to serve in local militias and maintain their weapons in the event they needed to be called into action. The purpose being to save the expense of garrisoning British Regulars in the colonies. A few years later, however, the regular army was once again required to quell the uprising in the colonies, known of course as the Revolutionary War. The colonial militias were called into action, some as loyalists troops fighting for the British, and others as patriots fighting to free the colonies from British rule. John Sr. was among the patriots.

Despite being forty-five years old and at the high end of the prior age requirements, John served in the Revolutionary War in 1781 as part of the Chester County militia. At the time he served, Pennsylvania law, which varied by necessity from the former British requirements, established that all white men between the ages of 18 and 53 had to serve two months of militia duty on a rotating basis. He served in the 2nd Company 2nd Battalion as a private under Captain Daniel Griffith and commanding officer Lt. Col. Thomas Bull. It is not clear where and under what circumstances he served, but he does show up on the regular army payroll in September 1781 for a nine-day enlistment in the same company under Captain Michael Holman. The difference in the name of the captains is likely because officers could change during a tour of duty in the federal army. When that tour was over, the soldier would go back to his original position with his state militia.

September of 1781 was one of the most significant times in the entire war. The Siege of Yorktown took place from September 28 to October 19 of that year and was the last major engagement of the Revolutionary War, even though a peace agreement was not signed until 1783. It was also a time when maintaining enough enlisted men was a challenge, which could explain the militias being called up for nine-day enlistments to cover specific needs. No Pennsylvania militias were used at Yorktown, so it is likely that John's service included either frontier duty or serving as a guard at local supply depots or prisoner of war camps. It is interesting to note that on the regular army payroll reports, John Sr. was listed as "John Fertick," the first known use of the name Fertick by a family member. It was not until John's great-grandson, Jacob Jr., that the name Fertick was used permanently, so it is curious for it to show up in that setting.

Taking time away from home and the farm could be a hardship for members of the militia, so the law allowed individuals who were able to pay for a substitute to take their place. John Sr. did not pay for a substitute, and this could account in part for Michael Fertig's description of the family circumstances in his letter to Lorenz Albert. He said John had a wife and six children but added that he "is not getting on" despite having one hundred acres of land. Census data can be used to gather information on family situations and often show ups and downs typical of the time. For example, in 1774 John had 30 acres, one horse, two cattle and three sheep. In 1777, he owned 100 acres. In 1780 he owned 72 acres and in 1782 owned 132. The numbers show a lot of variation over time, but in 1787 he owned 190 acres, three horses and four cattle so things appeared to be looking up.

Gustave Anjou recorded that in 1792, John Sr. purchased 182 acres from Tom Willing and in 1794 purchased 30 more from Henry Houpt. Anjou referred to John Sr. by the title Gentleman, possibly accurate but also possibly aiming for the status he liked to create. He implied that the Fertig family was connected by marriage to the Haupt/Houpt family, which was proven false, but the financial connection could be true. In 1797, John Sr. purchased 190 acres from an attorney named Robert Morris and in 1803 sold 98 acres to John Painter. He also gave his son, Abraham, 30 acres in 1805. At this point he was nearly seventy years old, and his remaining transactions show a man preparing to settle down.

Gravesite for John and Elizabeth Fertig, the first immigrants to America, at Brownback's Cemetery.

In Michael Fertig's letter to Lorenz Albert, he stated that he and John's mother had passed away in 1780. Michael passed on May 11, 1799, and was buried at Mount Pleasant Cemetery in Dauphin County, Pennsylvania. John's wife, Elizabeth, passed away on July 4, 1812, and was buried at Brownback's Cemetery in Chester County. The next year, John sold 113 acres to his son Jacob, the cost of which included an annual rent to be paid back to him. He also sold 70 acres to John Beerbower, his son-in-law and wife of Elizabeth, for a price that also included an annual rent. It appears that John Sr. was passing on his lands to his family while also securing rent to live off in his old age.

John Fertig, the original immigrant, passed away on January 13, 1831, at the ripe old age of ninety-four years old. He is buried next to Elizabeth at Brownback's Cemetery and has a marker next to his grave, still in place, letting future generations know that he was a Revolutionary War veteran. His tombstone reads:

In memory of John Fertig who was born in Europe the 24th of February in the Year of our Lord 1736. He came to America in the year 1754 and departed this life on the 13th of January A.D. 1831 aged 94 years 10 months and 11 days.

There was a time that time is past. When youth I bloomed like thee. A time will come Tis coming fast: That though shall fade like me.

Medallion at John Fertig's grave showing that he was a Revolutionary War veteran.

John Jr.

John Fertig Jr. was born on July 2, 1763, the first of seven children. Like his father, he served in the 2nd Battalion of the Chester County militia, albeit in the 1st Company under Captain Abraham Beatty. Like his father, he was ordered on a tour of duty on September 24, 1781; probably the same 9-day enlistment. This would confirm his 1763 birth year discussed in the last chapter and rule out 1768. Having turned eighteen only two months prior, he would have just qualified under Pennsylvania law to join his father in the militia. Four years later, in 1785, he married Margaretha Aughe.

Margaretha was born on April 21, 1756, in Chester County, the same county of birth as John Jr. She is likely part of the same family that produced Harmon Aughe, who married John's sister Mary. The Aughe name, like the Fertig name, can be found with various spellings such as Aughy or Ache, with different records showing the same person with different spellings. These variations often add more confusion to the Fertig family tree as it grew and included other families, as large families produced children who also have large families and often use the same common names over subsequent generations. Some well-intentioned but awkward connections result, made by over-enthusiastic internet genealogists as will be exemplified shortly with John Jr.'s son, another John.

John and Margaretha had four children together. As usual, some of the dates are unclear, though accurate enough to establish a history. Their first child was Henry, born on June 13, 1786. The second was a daughter, Sarah, born in 1790. The direct descendant in the line being followed here is the third child, Jacob, born on July 18, 1795. There is some debate on the fourth child, John. Some records show he was born in 1790, the same year as Sarah, but others show the more likely date of January 1, 1800. It was this John that eventually moved to Wayne County, Indiana, where the copy of Gustave Anjou's manuscript on the Fertig family was found by Pat Frappier in the Wayne County Library.

John and Margaretha helped found and build what is now known as the Old White Church near Ringtown, Pennsylvania. The Old White Church that still stands is unaltered other than a restoration completed in 1990, and is the same building built on the site in 1842. The original building John and Margaretha, and likely their children, helped build and establish was a log structure built on the same spot in 1810. Records show that many of John Jr.'s grandchildren and extended family were christened and baptized at the church. The cemetery at the church predates the building and it seems likely that several family members would be buried there, but only two are clear. Henry Fertig's first wife, Susanna, died on April

The Old White Church as it stands today in Ringtown, Pennsylvania.

The gravestones for Susanna Fertig and Abraham Fertig in the Old White Church Cemetery.

10, 1825. She was buried next to one of her sons, Abraham, who was born on February 15, 1820, and passed away on September 7, 1822.

Margaretha Fertig passed away sometime between 1815 and 1821, but the exact date is not known. Given that she was an active member of the Old White Church, it makes sense that she was buried there. Many of the tombstones are worn out beyond recognition, however, so it is impossible to say with certainty. John Jr. was remarried in 1822 to Katherine Gottschall. Their marriage is a good example of why it can be difficult to trust public genealogy websites, as hinted at above. One record indicates that John Jr.'s son, John, was the one to marry Katherine Gottschall, which is most certainly not accurate. That one error leads to long lists of siblings and connections in other genealogies that cannot be trusted but are still circulated online. John and Katherine did not have any other known children, and it is unlikely as she would have been around fifty years old at the time of their wedding.

John and Katherine stayed active at the Old White Church for a few more years according to church records announcing the births and christenings of their grandchildren. At some point they moved slightly north to Sugarloaf Township in Luzerne County, Pennsylvania. It was there that John Jr. passed away on March 31, 1840. A local German language newspaper printed an obituary for him.

> *"31 March 1840 Sugarloaf Twp., Luzerne County – John Fertig one time inhabitant of Union Township, Schuylkill County served in the Revolutionary War, was a honored citizen and treasured by all who knew him. April 1 his bones were laid to rest at the cemetery at Frieden's Church. May his ashes rest in peace."*

Frieden's Church is now Mountain Grove Lutheran Church in Bloomsburg. His tombstone stands apart from others in the cemetery with no other family nearby. Unlike his father, John Sr., who's tombstone listed him as John and was written in English, John Jr.'s tombstone was written in German. It is amazingly well preserved. Whether he preferred to have it written in German, or whether it was Katherine's idea is unknown. She had a hand with what was written. It reads:

> *A memorial to the love of Katherina,*
> *Born Gottschall*
> *For her last husband Johannes Fertig*
> *Born Sep 6 1763.*
> *In his first marriage he fathered with*
> *Margaretha Ache – 4 children,*
> *Grandchildren and great-grandchildren.*
> *We will meet on the other side.*

The tombstone of John Fertig Jr. is written in German and still in excellent condition.

Katherine was not buried near John. Her final resting place is unknown. She was last known to be living with her brother, Andrew, in Rush Township, Schuylkill County, in 1850.

Before moving on to the next Fertig in the line, a quick reference to the line of John Jr.'s brother, Abraham, will introduce a Fertig landmark. Abraham and his wife, Susanna, had a son named Isaac Fertig in 1807. Isaac and his wife, Hannah, had a son named John Fertig who was born on March 17, 1837. He was a successful businessman who went into politics, serving as mayor of Titusville, Pennsylvania, from 1873 to 1875 and elected to the Pennsylvania State Senate, serving from 1877 to 1878. John made his money in the oil industry. His home, built in 1872, still stands in Titusville. It is a beautiful home built in what is known as Italianate style and is a historic landmark in the town, known locally as the John Fertig House.

The John Fertig House in Titusville, Pennsylvania.

Jacob Sr.

Jacob Fertig Sr. was born on July 18, 1795. He is the first of two consecutive Jacobs in the line leading to Jerecho. While there is not much information to be found about either other than their long lists of children, they represent the final transition from Fertig to Fertick. The names are interchangeable at times, so there is no specific event that points to a conscious and permanent change, but it appears that it was during Jacob Jr.'s life that the Fertick name became official. Jacob Sr. was likely buried under the name Fertig, and when Jacob Jr. passed away, he was recorded as Fertick. A walking tour of a section of the cemetery in White Haven, Pennsylvania, was a shot in the dark attempt to find their graves. Later evidence indicated that it probably is the correct cemetery, so hopefully a future trip with a more dedicated search will find the tombstones of both men to see what valuable information they provide.

Jacob Sr. was married to Susanna Frey, sometimes shown as Fry, in 1821. Susanna was born on April 5, 1802, to William Abraham and Sophia Frey in Earl Township, Pennsylvania. Jacob and Susanna had at least eight children together. Their first child, William, was christened in the Old White Church on June 30, 1822, and likely born earlier that year or in late 1821. At the time, when a child was christened, the parents would present the child and would have sponsors as witnesses. William's sponsor was his grandfather and original church founder, John Fertig Jr. Their second child was Sarah Fertig who was born on Christmas Day, 1822, and christened on April 27, 1823, at the Old White Church like her older brother. Her sponsors were Jesse Hart and Sarah Frey, Susanna's sister who was single at the time. Both sponsors would play a role later in Jacob Jr.'s life.

The third child was Catherine who was born February 18, 1824, and christened in the same church as her siblings on April 18, 1824. She does not appear on every genealogy, but this is an oversight because she does show up in the 1880 Census living in White Haven as a single dressmaker. Jacob Jr. was the fourth child, born on April 7, 1825. He may have been the last of the children to be christened in the Old White Church. He was sponsored by his mother and the Reverend Binninger on June 26, 1825.

Another view of the Old White Church.

Some confusion regarding the actual number of children that Jacob and Susanna had begins with the fifth child. Genealogical information passed down to the family shows seven children but concedes that there are unusual gaps where others may have been born. One of those gaps can be filled by Charles who was likely born in 1828, making him the fifth child. The 1870 Census records a Charles Fertick living in White Haven and shows his relatives, including his parents, with the same last name. The 1850 Census shows the same names, but Charles and his parents having their last name listed as

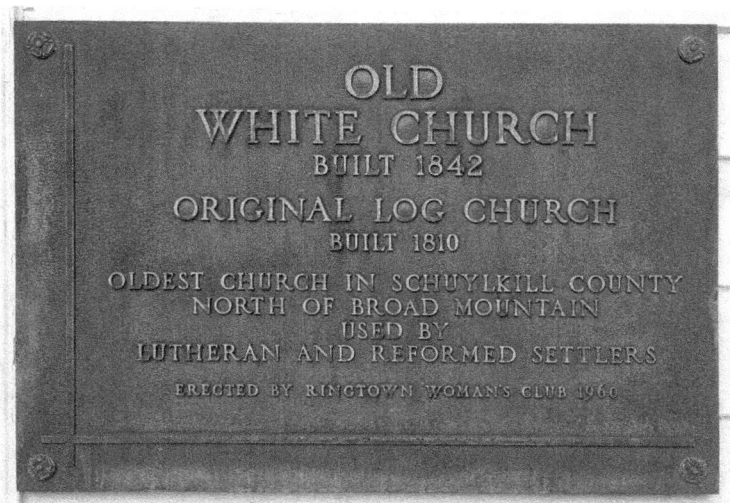

Plaque on the Old White Church commemorating its founding.

Festick, and siblings as Fustick. The constant misspellings were common, so it is conceivable that the change from Fertig to Fertick was a result of poor penmanship. The tombstones also changed from Fertig to Fertick, however, so it still seems to have been a conscious decision to eventually stay with Fertick.

The sixth child was Margaretha. Her date of birth is assumed to have been in 1831, but 1850 Census records show the date as 1832. Some records show two children, a Mary and a Margaret as the sixth and seventh children. The birth and death dates, however, are virtually identical so it is fairly certain that both refer to Margaretha. Mary Fertig was a common name found in several Fertig branches, so occasional confusion is understandable. A marriage record from October 26, 1853, shows Margaret Fertig, daughter of Jacob and Susan Fertig, marrying Emanuel Stivers in Wilkes-Barre, Pennsylvania, which is not far from White Haven. It is safe to say that this is the only Margaret, Mary, or Margaretha born to Jacob and Susan-

Trinity Church, now Mountain Grove Lutheran Church, where some of Jacob Sr.'s children were baptized and John Jr. is buried. It was known as Frieden's Church at the time of his burial.

na. Margaretha was christened at the Trinity Church, which is now Mountain Grove Lutheran. John Fertig Jr. was buried at that church, so it makes sense that the family's eventual move slightly north happened around the time of Margaretha's birth.

The seventh child was Henrianda, or Harriet, born on May 22, 1840, and christened at Mount Zion Union Church in Nescopeck, Pennsylvania. Her sponsors were Susanna's brother, Jacob Frey, and his wife Hanna. The eighth child was Karolina, born on August 9, 1842, in Mountain Grove and probably christened in the same church there as Margaretha. That is not certain, but it is in the same town where Trinity Church is found, and John Jr. was buried. Adding to that likelihood, the sponsor was Catherine Fertig, John Jr.'s widow.

Based on the information available, it appears that Jacob and Susanna had eight children. There is a reference to a Rebecca Fertig as a possible additional child, but that has absolutely no sources and is therefore speculation. It is best to stick to what is known or at least most likely. Rebecca Fertig is referring to one of Jacob and Susanna's daughter-in-laws, and that will become clearer in the next chapter on Jacob Jr.

Jacob Sr. and Susanna were known to have lived near White Haven according to census data from 1870 and 1880, and White Haven comes up often when following their children. Beyond the children, however, Jacob Sr. can be a hard person to find in any records. He passed away on February 2, 1881, at the age of eighty-five. It would make sense that he is buried in the cemetery at White Haven or somewhere in the vicinity, but the location is still a mystery. Susanna's final resting place is also unknown, but hopefully if one is found the other will be there with it.

8

Jacob Jr.

Jacob Fertick Jr. was born on April 7, 1825. He was the first in the line to go by the last name Fertick on a permanent basis but there is no clear time for when the family made that change. The name Fertick appeared from time to time going back to John Sr.'s Revolutionary War payroll records, but always came back to Fertig. Jacob Jr.'s tombstone has not been located yet, but his second wife was buried as Fertick, so at some point it was a conscious decision. Why did the name change to Fertick and stay that way? It has been speculated that the family wished to sound less German. This seems unlikely as there were no world events that would clearly make the family want to hide their heritage as may have been the case later during World Wars I and II. It seems especially unlikely in Eastern Pennsylvania with its large German population.

Like his mother and father, Jacob Jr. had a large family. His first wife was Rebecca Hart. She was born on October 5, 1833, in Ringtown to Jesse and Sarah Hart and christened in the Old White Church. Prior to their marriage, Jesse Hart and Sarah Frey were the sponsors at the christening of Jacob Jr.'s sister, Sarah in 1823. The last chapter mentioned some records showing Rebecca Fertig as a possible ninth child of Jacob Sr., but she was his daughter-in-law. Jacob and Rebecca had one child, Amanda, born on August 23, 1854. Rebecca passed away on January 28, 1856, and was buried in Bucks County, Pennsylvania, under the last name Fertig.

Amanda Fertig can be found in several of the family census records from the 1800s, which show she was single. A news article from the *Wilkes-Barre Times Leader* dated March 12, 1913, reported that she suffered severe burns a few days prior while at the home of her cousin, Lillian Kolb. Her clothes caught fire after touching a gas stove. The article indicated that she was recovering rapidly, but there must have been complications, because she passed away the day after it was printed, on March 13, 1913. At the time of her death, the article used the surname Fertick.

> Miss Amanda C. Fetrick, of Academy street, is at the City hospital making rapid recovery from burns received several days ago. She was at the home of her cousin, Miss Lillian Kolb, 58 Lehigh street, when her clothing became ignited from a gas stove. In trying to extinguish the blaze Miss Kolb was slightly burned.

Article in the Wilkes-Barre Times Leader *from March 12, 1913, reporting Amanda Fertick's accident prior to her death.*

Jacob Jr. married Susanna Lydia Zerfoss on December 5, 1860. She was born to Jonas and Susanna Zerfoss on October 10, 1842, making her seventeen years younger than Jacob. Family tradition has her going by Lydia and quite a few records show her as Lydia Susanna. Her tombstone, however, shows her name as Susanah L. Fertick, so her legal first name was Susanna. She probably went by Lydia to provide some distinction from her mother, with whom she shared a first name.

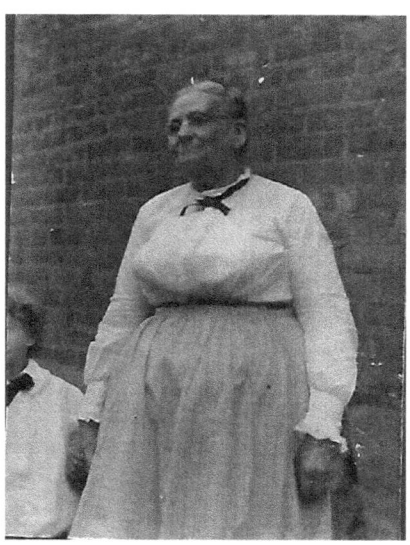

Lydia Fertick with her grandson, Roscoe Sr.

Lydia is the source of several family tales. The first is that she was of Native American descent. This is based on a picture from the early 1900s that certainly hints at a darker skin tone. She is shown in the picture with her grandson, Roscoe Sr., who also passed on the tradition that she was half Native American. Her mother's maiden name was Siegfried, so there are no clues to her origin to be found there. There is little reason to doubt the memories of the then young Roscoe Sr. as he had in-person access to his grandmother, but unfortunately no census or other records have been found to help confirm this. Another story passed down and responsible for an occasional snicker over the years is that Jacob Jr. would occasionally come home drunk, and an angry Lydia would hit him with a frying pan to show her displeasure. There is, of course, no way to verify this story, but it is an amusing anecdote that has made the rounds for well over one hundred years at this point.

Jacob and Lydia had eleven children, three of whom passed away at a young age. Frank was their first child, born in December of 1861. Their second child was Emma who was born in 1862, presumably late in the year. Harriet was born third in December of 1866 and Charles was the fourth, born one year later in December of 1867.

The 1870s proved to be a difficult time for Jacob and Lydia as their next three children were the ones who died young. Ida was born on January 10, 1870, and passed away on May 7 of the same year. Infant mortality was high in those days and explains why some families had a lot of children. The cause of death for Ida is unknown. Jacob Eric was born on April 29, 1871, and John was born on February 4, 1874. It is an unfortunate curiosity that both died just five days apart; Jacob on October 20, 1874, when he was three years old, and John on October 25 when he was only six months old. The records available do not give any indication of the cause of death and whether they were somehow related, but it was clearly a sad series of events for Jacob and Lydia.

They had four more children following those losses. William was born on August 21, 1875, Ario was born on January 4, 1878, and Stella on March 27, 1880. The youngest, Albert Lewis, was born on August 10, 1882, when Jacob Jr. was fifty-seven years old and just

Laurel Cemetery in White Haven, Pennsylvania, where Jacob Sr. and Jacob Jr. may be buried. (photo: Tom Wildoner)

before Lydia turned forty. Not much is known about Jacob and Lydia beyond their large family. The census in 1880 listed his occupation as laborer and the family was always located in the same general vicinity of Luzerne County that included Sugarloaf Township, White Haven, and Wilkes-Barre, which is where the next in the line, Albert, spent most of his life.

Jacob Jr. passed away on June 10, 1901, in Wilkes-Barre, Pennsylvania, and was buried in White Haven. Lydia was still living in Wilkes-Barre in 1910, but eventually relocated to Johnstown, Pennsylvania. Her son, Ario, was living in Johnstown in 1917 according to his draft registration form, so it is likely that she was living with him or near him at the time of her death on October 13, 1915, just a few days past her seventy-third birthday. She was buried there in Grandview Cemetery.

Lydia's gravesite in Johnstown, Pennsylvania.

Albert

Albert Lewis Fertick was born on August 10, 1882, and was the youngest of the eleven children Jacob Jr. and Lydia had together. He was born in Jonesville, Pennsylvania, which is in Carbon County. His obituary says he was born in Jamestown, Pennsylvania, but that is in the far western part of the state, so Jonesville appears to be the more likely birthplace. He married Mabel Kolb who was born in Weatherly, Pennsylvania, also part of Carbon County. Mabel was born on July 2, 1885, the daughter of Lewis and Mary Kolb. She and Albert were married on September 16, 1903, in Binghamton, New York.

The Fertig, eventually Fertick, family and the Kolb family seem to have been familiar long before Albert and Mabel were married.

Albert and Mabel Fertick.

When perusing Fertig family records, the Kolb family shows up relatively often. In the 1913 news article about the injuries sustained by Amanda Fertick in the fire that ultimately claimed her life, she was reported to be visiting the home of her cousin, Lillian Kolb, at the time of the accident. Lillian suffered from minor injuries in the incident while trying to assist her.

Albert and Mabel had three children together. The oldest was Roscoe, eventually Roscoe Sr., who was born on August 8, 1904. Roscoe was the first of three generations that produced only one son, so the Fertick name is much easier to trace from this point on as the families were not as large. Their second child, Margaret, was born on September 22, 1906. The third and last child, June, was born on March 5, 1917. All the children were born in Wilkes-Barre where Albert and Mabel spent their entire married life.

During his lifetime, Albert worked as a painter and wallpaper hanger. When he retired, he was working as a drill press operator for WH Nicholson & Company, which manufactured equipment for power plants. He and Mabel attended First Evangelical United Brethren Church. Soon after he passed away, the church merged with another to form the current Albright United Methodist Church of which Mabel remained a member until her death twenty-one years later. Albert was also active in several community groups, including the Sons and Daughters of Liberty and the Junior Order of United American Mechanics.

Albert and his family participated in a variety of community events over the years. He and at least three of his brothers were part of a singing group that performed locally and occasionally in Philadelphia. A picture of the group shows eight men in total. Someone has placed a mark on four of the eight men in the picture, all in the bottom row, and the family resemblance is clear. Brothers Ario and William are next to each other on the left side of the picture. Next to them sits their

Music group featuring four of the Fertick brothers. From left to right in the front row, Ario, William, Charles and Albert (just behind William and Charles).

brother Charles, and just behind Charles is Albert. If not for Charles' mustache, he and Albert would be nearly indistinguishable. The identities of the other four men in the picture are unknown.

Another memory that has been passed down is that Albert's daughter, June, worked for the Hershey Chocolate factory in Hershey, Pennsylvania. Not surprisingly, this memory comes from Albert's grandson and June's nephew, Roscoe Jr., because what kid is not going to have some vivid memories of the treats that his aunt would bring home from work in a chocolate factory.

Albert passed away on December 5, 1956, after suffering a hemorrhagic stroke at the age of seventy-four. He was buried in the Memorial Shrine Cemetery in Carverton, Pennsylvania, just outside of Wilkes-Barre. Mabel lived for another two decades before passing away from heart disease on February 7, 1977, at the age of ninety-one. She was buried with Albert in the Memorial Shrine Cemetery.

Albert and Mabel continued the tradition of the family living in Pennsylvania, having lived there for their entire lives. It was their son, Roscoe, who eventually moved out of Pennsylvania when he answered the call of his country to serve in the military during the 1940s and the outbreak of World War II. Following the war, this line of the Fertick family began to move west.

Albert Fertick later in life.

Family picture. From left to right, front row, Mabel, Albert, and Roscoe Jr. with his two aunts, June and Margaret. In the back row, Charles Roberts, his wife Erma, Roscoe Sr. and Joyce Fertick.

10

Roscoe Sr.

Roscoe Lewis Fertick Sr. was born in Wilkes-Barre on August 4, 1904. It was there that he met and married his first wife, Rachel Cook, in 1927. According to their marriage application, she was eleven years older, but future census records show various age gaps. They did not have any children, and it appears they were married until the early 1940s when Roscoe left Wilkes-Barre for Washington, DC, to serve on active duty after three years in the U.S. Navy Reserve.

Roscoe Sr. did not take the traditional route of joining the military out of high school or college. In the 1930s, however, as expectations grew that a new war was inevitable and would eventually draw the United States into the conflict, Roscoe made the decision to serve his country. On March 16, 1938, he joined the U.S. Naval Reserve, working as a radioman for the Fourth Naval District in Philadelphia. He was a HAM radio operator, so working in Naval Communications was a natural fit. He was recognized for passing his Naval Communications correspondence course

Roscoe Sr.'s official Navy picture.

with distinction and rose to the rank of Petty Officer 2nd Class. He was the petty officer in charge of the local Radio Reserve radio station where he continued to serve at a high level and was recognized for his exceptional performance.

In April of 1940, a historic storm produced flooding along the Susquehanna River and hit Wilkes-Barre especially hard, causing several bridges to collapse and thousands of residents to be evacuated. Roscoe's reserve unit volunteered to assist with communications and by all accounts performed admirably. After the floods subsided, Roscoe received letters of commendation from the American Red Cross and from the commandant of the Fourth Naval District. In November of the same year, he received a letter from the Navy Department informing him that based on the recommendation of his District Communications Officer, he was being mobilized into active duty in the Communications Security Section in Washington, DC. He was instructed to immediately start courses in cryptanalysis, and on July 7, 1941, five months to the day before Pearl Harbor, Roscoe arrived in Washington, DC, and was sworn into active duty.

During his time working in DC Roscoe met and married his second wife, Mary Joyce Roberts. Joyce, as she preferred to be called, was born in Spencer, Iowa, to E. Joy and Lena Roberts on April 22, 1911. This was also the second marriage for Joyce. She had one child from her first marriage, Charles Dean James,

Roscoe Sr. and Joyce.

born on May 1, 1932. Going by Dean, he would also join the military, serving with distinction as an officer and helicopter pilot during the Vietnam War. Prior to his Army service and during Joyce's time working for the Navy Department in Washington, DC, Dean lived with her parents in Spencer. Her father, Joy, was a well-known resident in Spencer, spending nearly forty years acting as the town's unofficial Santa Claus, collecting toys throughout the year, and delivering them to needy children at Christmas. There is a monument commemorating him still in a local park in Spencer.

Roscoe and Joyce had one child, Roscoe Lewis Jr., who was born on June 14, 1943, while both worked in the Navy Department. When his military service was up, Roscoe Sr. worked as a painter and undertook restoration projects in several historic buildings, including the

Roscoe Sr. and Roscoe Jr. on their front porch in Washington, DC.

Dumbarton Oaks Estate in Georgetown. In 1948, President Harry S. Truman authorized an extensive renovation of the White House that lasted for four years. Roscoe Sr. was a painter during the renovation and oversaw the matching of colors. On one occasion, rushing to a worksite while carrying two gallons of paint, he came around a corner and almost ran into Bess Truman. Fortunately, he was stopped by the Secret Service just prior to dousing the First Lady in paint.

Another time while working in DC, Roscoe was tasked with painting a mural in a local Ethiopian restaurant. A large black car pulled up in front of the restaurant and the Emperor of Ethiopia, Haile Selassie, stepped into the restaurant and recognizing the landscape on the mural, asked Roscoe when he had been in his country. He replied that he had never been there and showed the Emperor an Ethiopian postage stamp that he was using as his model.

Roscoe Sr. was also an artist and painted several pictures, many of which are still hanging on the walls of the homes of his son and grandchildren to this day. Between the time he got out of the military and 1960, Roscoe and his family moved from time to time between Washington, DC, and Joyce's hometown of Spencer, Iowa. They also spent time living in Sioux Falls, South Dakota, which is just across the Iowa border and not far from Spencer. In 1960, the family moved across the country to Salem, Oregon, and Roscoe's son, grandchildren and great-grandchildren have lived in or near Oregon ever since.

On April 19, 1964, Roscoe Sr. passed away unexpectedly from coronary thrombosis, or a blood clot that formed in his heart. Joyce stayed in Salem after her husband passed away and was joined there by her brother, Charles Roberts, who she called Buddy and her grandchildren referred to as Unc. In 1988 while visiting Roscoe Jr. and his family, Joyce suffered a stroke and passed away on July 21.

She was buried next to her husband and her brother, who had preceded her, in City View Cemetery in Salem.

Roscoe Sr. working on one of his last paintings. The painting, currently displayed in Roscoe Jr.'s living room, was nearly complete when he passed away and one can still see areas on the rocks and trees that are incomplete.

Roscoe Jr.

Roscoe Fertick Jr. was born in Washington, DC, on June 14, 1943. He was the only child of Roscoe Sr. and Joyce. Early in his life, the family moved often, so Roscoe Jr. spent time as a child in Washington, DC, Spencer, and Sioux Falls, never spending more than three years at any one school. There are pictures showing a very young Roscoe watching his grandfather, Joy Roberts, working in his toy shop in Spencer with the intense interest to be expected from a young child in such a fascinating environment.

Winters in Spencer can be cold and harsh. One of the stories that Roscoe Jr. passed down over the years was an unfortunate event that occurred when he went out one day in below-freezing temperatures. While walking on the ice of the Little Sioux River looking for frozen catfish, he was joined by a pack of local dogs that liked to follow him around on his adventures. One dog got too close to him, and the extra weight caused the ice to break, dropping Roscoe into the frigid river. Fortunately, he was able to get out and walk home to the warmth and care of his family. They helped him slide out of his cold, soaked pants, which they then stood upright near the fireplace. His pants were frozen solid.

Roscoe Jr. has always been an outdoorsman at heart. Certificates from Camp Foster in Spirit Lake, Iowa, show that by fourteen he was becoming proficient in riflery and archery. He enjoyed hunting early in life, but his first love has always been fishing and that has continued through the present day. He also practiced falconry at one point and wrote about falconry references in Shakespeare while in college at Oregon College of Education (OCE), now Western Oregon University. His findings were later published in the academic journal *The Explicator,* put out by Virginia Commonwealth University. This occurred, of course, after the family had moved west to Salem, Oregon.

Roscoe started his senior year of high school in Washington, DC, but one month later he and his parents moved to Salem. He would finish his senior year attending North Salem High School. While in DC, he enlisted in the National Guard on his seventeenth birthday and when he was eighteen years old, went to boot camp immediately after graduation. He spent six and a half years in the guard before he left the service to begin a career in law enforcement.

Roscoe Jr. and his mother, Joyce, at his National Guard boot camp graduation.

Roscoe graduated from high school in 1961. One of the first people he met at North Salem was Billie Harris, who he brazenly swatted on her backside by way of introduction. The questionable introduction aside, the two became friends and occasionally dated. Billie was the second of four children of Ray and Althea Harris. The relationship grew and the two were married on February 16, 1965, not long after Roscoe Sr. had passed away. After their marriage,

Roscoe Jr. and Billie Harris were married on February 16, 1965, in Salem, Oregon.

Roscoe started working at the Oregon State Penitentiary as a guard, and after finishing his Criminal Justice degree from OCE in 1972, started the career he would eventually retire from as a parole officer.

Roscoe and Billie have three children together, all born in Salem. Their first child, Lisa, was born on October 29, 1966, followed fourteen months later by their first and only son, Scott, born on January 14, 1968. Their last child, Shannon, was born on October 30, 1971. The family moved to Springfield, Oregon, around 1974 where Roscoe continued his criminal justice career. At one point, Roscoe managed a work-release program located in an old rundown house in downtown Eugene near the University of Oregon campus. From a work perspective, the house is not very memorable, but to pop culture fanatics, the outside of the house is easily recognizable as the notorious fraternity Delta Tau Chi from the classic movie comedy, Animal House, filmed in 1978.

In the 1980s, Roscoe Jr. felt called to the ministry and started a church in Eugene named Maranatha Baptist Church. After a short time there, he left his criminal justice career and the family moved back to Salem so he could attend Western Conservative Baptist Seminary to further his new career. While living in Salem, Roscoe got the opportunity to show off his fishing prowess on a local television show called "Fishing the West" with host Larry Shoenborn. Roscoe was the guest on a show about flyfishing for rockfish at night off the jetty in Newport, Oregon. While filming the show, Roscoe learned that Larry was planning another episode where he would take a child fishing for shad. As a result of that conversation, Roscoe's youngest daughter, Shannon, was selected and filmed her own episode of the show a few months later.

After two years in Salem, the family returned to the Eugene area and Roscoe became the pastor of Dexter Baptist Church in Dexter, Oregon. In an ironic twist, a famous scene from the movie Animal

Family portrait from the mid 1980s.

House takes place in the Dexter Lake Club near the family's residence. The family seemed destined to be around filming locations from that movie. While the movie is certainly not family friendly, watching it can be a trip down memory lane, especially for Roscoe's son Scott, who attended the University of Oregon where much of the movie was filmed. After a few years in Dexter, Roscoe felt criminal justice was still his calling and returned to his career as a parole officer, first in Roseburg and then settling in Tillamook, Oregon, where he and Billie reside to this day.

While working in Tillamook, Roscoe still took time to teach in his local church and enjoy the many fishing opportunities available in the area. He retired from Tillamook County Corrections in 2010, but has, of course, continued to teach and fish. Roscoe and Billie currently enjoy eight grandchildren and three great-grandchildren and having a home on the coast to entertain their children and their children's families. They have been married for fifty-nine years and are looking forward to number sixty.

Roscoe Jr. holding a trophy bass caught at Clear Lake, California.

12

Scott

Scott Fertick was born on January 14, 1968, in Salem, Oregon, where he lived for the first six years of his life. Despite young memories being hard to come by sometimes, he remembers very clearly looking forward to noon every Saturday when a local television station would play their "Creature Feature," where he developed a lifelong love of Godzilla. Even as an adult, and with Godzilla movies still coming out regularly, Scott owns all the Godzilla movies ever made and continues to share that fandom with his own family.

When the family moved to Springfield, Oregon, Scott picked up another lifelong passion, this time for soccer. He started playing soccer in the third grade and continued to play through high school and for various recreational leagues into adulthood. Scott played soccer at Pleasant Hill High School while the family lived in Dexter and graduated from that school in 1986. After high school, he attended the University of Oregon for two years. College was not the priority it should have been at that time, but Scott did make the most of his summers. In 1986 he worked at Cannon Beach Conference Center in Cannon Beach, Oregon, and in 1987 was the last manager at the very run-down Eugene Drive-In before it shut down permanently. In 1988, he spent the summer living and working as a camp counselor in Soldotna, Alaska, at Solid Rock Bible Camp.

As Scott grew up fishing, camping and occasionally hunting he developed a love of nature. In Alaska, an event occurred that added to his respect for nature, and especially for large bears. While hiking with a friend in the tundra of Denali National Park, the two of them separated to opposite sides of a small rise hoping to get a picture of two caribou they had spotted. Scott thought he heard a noise behind him, and already somewhat nervous about bears, turned to see an extremely large grizzly running directly at him. The bear was not looking at Scott but looking behind as if startled. When the grizzly finally looked forward and saw Scott it slid to a quick stop, dust flying from its skid. The two sat staring at each other in uncomfortably close proximity.

Noticing a small decline to his left, Scott slowly moved down until out of the bear's vision, and then quickly left the tense situation. Fortunately, the bear did not follow, and Scott was able to locate his friend hiding in tall grass on the opposite side of the rise. Apparently, his friend had seen the bear and dove for cover, spooking the bear, which then ran straight at Scott. Soon after, the two hikers spotted the caribou they had been searching for, just in time to see the same bear run out of the bush chasing the two animals. It was all the motivation they needed, realizing that the bear was hunting, to run to the nearest road and get as much distance from the tundra as possible. No more hiking on that trip, but they both left Alaska with a great story to tell and a long-term irrational fear of bears.

In 1989, realizing college was not working out, Scott joined the Navy and attended Naval Nuclear Power School, qualifying as an electrician on the nuclear-powered ship, USS *Truxtun* (CGN-35). He was stationed in Bremerton, Washington, and went on two deployments to the Persian Gulf and various other excursions. During his six years in the service, Scott visited many foreign ports. In Asia, he made port calls in Hong Kong, the Philippines, Singapore,

Scott's Navy boot camp picture from 1989.

Scott playing a friendly game of soccer for his ship in Australia in 1993.

and Thailand. In the Middle East he stopped in Bahrain, Oman, United Arab Emirates, and Saudi Arabia. He even spent a few days in Djibouti on the African continent and Australia. Back in the western hemisphere he transited the Panama Canal and made stops in Panama, Curacao, Columbia and managed to make a phone call from a phone booth at the end of a dock in Cuba, just to say he had been there.

While living in Bremerton, Scott met Kathryn Rebecca Probst and the two were married on January 8, 1994, at Faith Fellowship in Silverdale, Washington. Kathryn is the daughter of Herbert Eugene (Gene) and Valerie Probst. She was born on February 11, 1973, in Scarborough, England. Her mother was from England and her father was an American working abroad. Kathryn and her siblings, Esther and Nick, moved to America in 1979 with their parents and lived in Port Orchard, Washington, near Bremerton where she eventually met Scott. She graduated from South Kitsap High School in 1990.

When Scott separated from the Navy in 1995, he and Kathryn moved to the area around Portland, Oregon. Scott eventually returned to college, and taking it much more seriously this time, graduated from Portland State University in 2003 with a Bachelor of Arts degree in history. While initially Scott saw history only as a subject that might hold his interest while he achieved his real goal of getting a bachelor's degree for the sake of the degree, he found a real love of history and writing. For the last twenty years he has continued to read history and classics and that has resulted in a sizable personal library and a love of books. Immediately after graduating, he and Kathryn moved across the Columbia River to Vancouver, Washington.

Scott and Kathryn Probst were married on January 8, 1994, in Silverdale, Washington.

As this story has now come to a time when the family is still actively growing, it would be a benefit to touch on where the Fertick family has branched off. Scott's oldest sister, Lisa, married Marcus Humphries and the two of them had three children: Brandice who was born in 1988, Kevin in 1989, and Isaac in 1991. Brandice has two children of her own; Kyrie who was born in 2007 and Leyla in 2008. Shannon, Scott's youngest sister, married Vincent Rubeo from New York in 1991 and they have two children, Nick born in 1992 and Anthony Joseph (AJ) in 1995. Nick married Autumn Cole in 2022. An understanding of Scott and Kathryn's nieces and nephews will help to follow the growth of their own family.

Scott and Kathryn in 2015.

Scott and Kathryn broke the three-generation cycle of families having only one male child who might carry on the family name to future generations. Their first son, Jacob Max, was born on July 8, 1999, and their second, Noah Spencer, was born on February 5, 2002. Both boys were born in Tualatin, Oregon. Adding a third Jacob in the Fertig/Fertick family line was not a conscious decision, but it certainly followed a trend. Noah's middle name, Spencer, was a nod to his great, great-grandfather mentioned in a previous chapter, Joy Roberts, who lived in Spencer, Iowa. On June 7, 2006, Scott and Kathryn had their first daughter, Mia Amelia, named for soccer player Mia Hamm and Kathryn's grandmother, Esther Amelia. She was born after the family relocated to Vancouver, Washington.

Scott and Kathryn's fourth child, Kyrie Jubilee, was previously mentioned. She was born to Scott's niece, Brandice, on February 23, 2007, in Eugene, Oregon, and adopted in 2012 by Scott and

Kathryn. Due to her dual role for the children of Scott and Kathryn, Scott's sister, Lisa, as aunt to the first three children and grandmother to Kyrie, has been dubbed "Grantie" Lisa in the Fertick household. She has owned this title with a considerable amount of pride.

Scott and Kathryn still live in Vancouver. Scott works as an officer for the Transportation Security Administration and Kathryn works in home health care for Home Instead. Scott still has a love of books and all things Godzilla and would like to start writing more, just for the love of writing. A new favorite pastime for both Scott and Kathryn is hanging out with their first grandchild, Jerecho, of whom more will be written and who is in large part the motivation for writing this book. They enjoy seeing their kids growing and moving into or towards adulthood. They have been married for thirty years and plan on enjoying many more to come.

Jacob

Jacob Fertick was born on July 8, 1999, the first child of Scott and Kathryn and the first to potentially carry on the family name. For the first time since Albert, the family added a second son when Noah was born on February 5, 2002. Mia and Kyrie came around just a few years later and all will have their say in where the family name progresses in the future, but to date, Jacob is the only one who has continued the line. The others will gladly wait as they are still working on their educations and have more than enough time to determine their paths in life.

Jacob and Noah both played soccer and wrestled in their youth and into middle school. Upon entering high school, both switched

Jacob and Noah getting ready to cheer on their Oregon Ducks football team in 2010.

to cross country and track, and Jacob continued wrestling. Jacob eventually lettered in all three sports and Noah in track and cross country. Jacob also participated in band for all four years. Both graduated from Evergreen High School, Jacob in 2018 and Noah in 2020. Despite the two-year difference, both graduated with associate degrees from Clark College in 2020. Jacob was a traditional college student while Noah attended Clark for his last two years of high school through the Running Start program allowing him to earn his high school diploma and associate degree simultaneously, getting a head start on his four-year degree.

Mia and Kyrie were also students at Evergreen High School. Mia graduated on June 7, 2024, also her 18th birthday. While both played soccer and ran cross country when they were younger, neither pursued sports in high school. Mia found her passion for theater and was active all four years as a theater tech and occasional actor. She also loves writing and is currently looking at her college options to continue her education. Kyrie is going to be a senior for the 2024-25 school year. She has a natural affinity for art and fashion, but also has been considering a career in the medical field later in life.

Kathryn and her children. From left to right: Kyrie, Noah, Kathryn, Mia and Jacob.

After high school, Jacob worked summers at Cannon Beach Conference Center while attending Clark College. After getting his degree, he decided to work for a year as a conference assistant while attending Washington State University online. He eventually stopped attending WSU to focus on working full time. Noah started attending Seattle Pacific University after high school where he received his bachelor's degree in nutrition and dietetics. He has decided to continue his education and is currently working towards his master's degree in dietetics and completing his required internships at Cedar Crest College in Allentown, Pennsylvania. He is due to complete his program in 2025.

While in Cannon Beach, Jacob befriended two people who would have significant impacts on his life. For a time, he dated Joshlyn Schumacher and the two of them became proud parents of the newest member of the Fertick line, Jerecho Fertick Schumacher, who was born on January 12, 2022. While no longer in a relationship, Jacob and Joshlyn have been successfully co-parenting Jerecho, who

Jacob and Jerecho in 2022.

is a huge blessing to both families. Jacob also met Emma Lady when he first moved to Cannon Beach. The two became fast friends, and although they lost contact for a time, five years after meeting they reconnected and this time their friendship blossomed into much more.

Emma Geetika Lady was born in India along with her twin sister, Preetika. Preetika passed away as a baby, but Emma was adopted by her parents, Steve and Cheryl Lady, and brought to the United States where she lived in Phoenix, Arizona, eventually relocating to Spokane, Washington. When Emma and Jacob reconnected, it did not take long for them to see that their futures belonged together. Emma would say that she waited for five years for Jacob to come around, and when he did, there was no doubt. They were married on July 6, 2024, and reside in Vancouver to be near Jerecho.

Jacob has been working for the Veteran's Administration since returning home from Cannon Beach in 2021. He enjoys interacting with the veterans under his care and has the opportunity for a long, successful career working for the federal government should he choose. Emma worked as a prep cook at Cannon Beach Conference Center and regularly shows off her cooking talents, much to the culinary satisfaction of her new family. Emma and Jacob talk about their goal of sixty years together and there is no reason to think they will not succeed. Both are committed to their marriage and to Jerecho, not to mention any future siblings for Jerecho when the time is right. Emma is a welcome addition to the Fertick family.

Jacob and Emma Lady were married on July 6, 2024, in Vancouver, Washington.

14

Jerecho & the Future

Jerecho Fertick Schumacher was born on January 12, 2022, and represents the beginning of the next generation to follow the Fertick name. He is the first grandchild of both sets of his grandparents and is deeply loved by both the Fertick and the Schumacher families. This book is inspired in large part by Jerecho's arrival. For the Fertick family, the history from the immigrant, John Fertig, through the subsequent generations has been known, but has been tucked away on lists and documents stuffed in boxes or folders and never put into a clear, narrative form. It is the hope that this book will provide current and future generations of the Fertick clan a precise, easy-to-read history that can be added to by anyone in the future who wishes to do so.

Jerecho dressed to impress at the wedding of Jacob and Emma.

To Jerecho, his future siblings and cousins, and their future generations, it is the hope that you will always be aware of your family history and understand where you come from. You can rest assured that you are loved and that your entire family is looking forward to seeing you grow and create your own chapters for yourselves. For myself personally, the author, you have added and will continue to add so much to my life. You are my heart, and I look forward to all the time I am given to enjoy you and watch you shape your own stories to pass on in the future.

On one of Jerecho's first visits to grandma and grandpa's house, he and Scott wasted no time in sharing their mutual love of books.

Appendix

De La Ferte Family Tree by Gustave Anjou

Antoine De La Ferte
- Born – unknown
- Married in 1487 to Marguerite des Gardins in the Monastery of Maitenay, Pas-de-Calais
- Deceased around 1540

Francois De La Ferte
- Born – unknown
- Married on July 11, 1537, to Marie Leinau at the Castle of St. Omar
- Deceased around 1550/51

Guillaume de la Ferte
- Born in 1540 – Desvres, Pas-de-Calais, Nord-Pas-de-Calais, France
- Married on October 6, 1586, to Jeanne Barbey at the church of Notre Dame at St. Omar
- Deceased June 8, 1605 – Desvres, Pas-de-Calais, Nord-Pas-de-Calais, France; Age: 65 years old

Guillaume Ferte (alias Fertich)
- Born January 3, 1588 – Desvres, Pas-de-Calais, Nord-Pas-de-Calais, France
- Married on May 4, 1619, to Catherine Freneau
- Deceased November 2, 1668 – Beaumont, Dordogne, Aquitaine, France; Age: 80 years old

Pierre Ferte (Listed as Peter Fertig at death)
- Born March 11, 1620
- Married on February 17, 1666, to Alice Paul at the Hotel de ville, Charleville.
- Deceased August 24, 1693 – Frankenthal, Rhineland-Palatinate, Germany; Age: 73 years old

Johannes Paul Fertig (born Jean Ferte)
- Born January 3, 1667 – Beaumont, Dordogne, Aquitaine, France
- Moved with parents to Frankenthal, Rhineland-Palatinate prior to 1685
- Married on June 3, 1698, to Johanna Schneider
- Deceased May 5, 1725 – Diedesheim, Rhineland-Palatinate, Germany; Age: 58 years old

Adam Fertig
- Born February 4, 1700 – Rhineland-Palatinate, Germany
- Married on May 3, 1734, to Johanna Haupt
- Deceased February 3, 1761

John Fertig
- Born February 24, 1736 – Deidesheim, Bad Dürkheim, Rhineland-Palatinate, Germany
- Deceased January 13, 1831 – Vincent, Chester, Pennsylvania, United States; Age: 94 years old

www.ingramcontent.com/pod-product-compliance
Lightning Source LLC
Chambersburg PA
CBHW050041080526
44586CB00014B/1400